May Morton:
Phantom Poet

May Morton, Vienna, 1955

Liz McManus
Editor

MAY MORTON:
PHANTOM POET

ARLEN
HOUSE

May Morton: Phantom Poet

is published in 2026 by

ARLEN HOUSE
42 Grange Abbey Road
Baldoyle
Dublin D13 A0F3
Ireland
Email: arlenhouse@gmail.com
www.arlenhouse.ie

ISBN 978–1–85132–365–4, paperback

International distribution
SYRACUSE UNIVERSITY PRESS
621 Skytop Road, Suite 110
Syracuse
New York 13244–5290
USA
Email: supress@syr.edu
www.syracuseuniversitypress.syr.edu

© Liz McManus, 2026

Every reasonable effort has been made to trace copyright holders of material reproduced in this book, but if any have been inadvertently overlooked the publishers would be glad to hear from them

The moral right of the author has been asserted

Typesetting by Arlen House

Cover image:
Portrait of Miss May Morton by Eileen Ayrton
bequeathed to the Ulster Museum by the sitter in 1957

Contents

13   May Morton (1879–1957): A Phantom Poet
      Liz McManus

Dawn and Afterglow
37   Dawn
38   If I Had a Lover
40   The Oak, He is a Farming Man
42   Mountain Mist
43   My Pal
44   Boat Song
45   Snowdrops
46   Favourites
47   Afterglow
48   Recompense
49   Divided
50   Aftermath
51   A Thought
52   The Hidden Scroll
53   I Met a Friend
55   To Glenariff
57   Exiled
58   Lament of the Keening Women – Arranmore
59   Isle of Mist
61   Shadows
62   Round my Garden
63   The Test
64   Retrospect
66   Whither?

Masque in Maytime (1948)
71   Masque in Maytime

Spindle and Shuttle (1951)
81   Spindle and Shuttle

Sung to the Spinning Wheel (1952)
91   Singer-Spinner
92   The Book
93   The Pearl
94   Street Tapestry
95   There are Three Things
96   Women and Roses
97   To M.E.T.B of Townley Hall
98   Dedication of a Teacher
99   Ships
100 Moon-Spun
101 Song of the Wild Bees
102 The Gunner
103 The Bandit
104 The Conscript
105 To Her First Love
106 Love's Finest Hour
107 Fidelity
108 To Her Last Love
109 Discord
110 To a Barrage Balloon
111 Wings
112 We May Not Sing – We Dare Not Sleep
113 Blitzed
114 With Beak and Claw
115 Life's New Year
116 Easter – 1946
117 Oneless
118 The Poet
119 The Talisman
120 To the Author of *Flowers for a Lady*
121 The Path and the Goal

122	Silent
123	Elegy
124	Alone
125	Milestone
126	Farewell
127	The Rope
128	*Acknowledgements*
129	*About the Author*
130	*About the Editor*

In memory of
Victoria Amelina

During her visit to Dublin in October 2022, the young Ukrainian writer and PEN Ukraine representative, Victoria Amelina, addressed a large audience in Smock Alley Theatre. She spoke eloquently about poetry, about politics and about her work in documenting war crimes since the Russian invasion of Ukraine in February 2022. Nine months later, on 27 June 2023, Amelina was sitting with a group of Colombian writers in a pizza restaurant in the Ukrainian city of Kramatorsk when a Russian missile strike injured her so badly that she died in hospital four days later, at the age of thirty seven. Victoria Amelina is survived by her husband and twelve-year old son.

May Morton:
Phantom Poet

May Morton
(1879–1957):
A Phantom Poet

May Morton's last poetry collection was published in 1952, five years before she died. The final poem in that collection is entitled *The Rope*. It begins with the lines: 'A phantom rope, a shadow on the gray/moored fast to nothingness'. That ghostly image could be a metaphor for May Morton's life and death. During her lifetime she was a considerable force in the literary world around her, both in her writings and in her work for Irish PEN but, after she died, her reputation, over time, dwindled into obscurity.

Until recently it could be said that May Morton became a phantom poet. This book sets out to re-establish her position as an important Northern Irish poet who broke new ground in her writings and who left a legacy of essays and poetry that deserve to be remembered.

Diversity in Unity
> There must be diversity in unity and the greater the diversity the richer the unity [...] For Truth has many aspects. Its white ray is composed of many colours, not only primary and secondary but multitudinous as the rich complexity of the human soul.[1]

May Morton wrote these words in 1942, in her contributory essay to *The Writer and the PEN* in the first ever publication of the Belfast Centre of PEN. Her thesis that "The greater the diversity the richer the unity" has a startlingly modern ring to it. Today a plea for tolerance and inclusion based on the rainbow image is familiar. It is vividly captured, for example, in the flag of the LGBTQ+ community. Over eighty years ago, however, in wartime Belfast, it was a radical argument for a woman writer to make.

A superficial impression of May Morton is of a quiet-living spinster and retired teacher who lived with her sister in a respectable suburb of Belfast and made herself useful as secretary for a number of literary societies. Her work tells a different story: her early poems express a latent sexual desire. In Morton's first collection, *Dawn and Afterglow* (1937), she writes highly-romanticised poems about the Ulster landscape. In one poem titled *To Glenariff* her images are frankly sensual:

> The sun shall softly throw upon your
>   couch his golden spears,
> And kiss your heavy eyelids, shadowed
>   with the mountain's tears [...]
>
> And I shall hear your laughter where the
>   stream runs swift and clear
> And feel your fragrant breath upon my
>   cheek, your soul so near
> That it shall stoop on shining wings to
>   bless some quiet pool

> Where languid ferns with long green fingers
>   touch the waters cool
> While its pure flame, enshrined in solitude,
>   remote, divine,
> Shall merge its whiteness in the redder
>   glow that burns in mine (pp 58–59).

According to Richard Kirkland in *The Poetics of Partition: Poetry and Northern Ireland* (2012) another early poem of Morton's from that collection, *Mountain Mist*, encapsulates an "erotically charged delight in the Ulster countryside."

> Maiden of the mountain mist,
> Stooping boldly to be kissed
> When the young and ardent sun
> First pursues you – half in fun,
> Wherefore snatch your robe of grey
> From his grasp and haste away
> When his passion's hot desire
> Follows you with lips of fire? (p. 27).

Isle of Mist, a poem in the same collection, displays the same "erotically charged delight."

> Soft now, the June night calls: and sea and sky
> Shall know you for the wanton that you are!
> Enamoured of your fiery paramour
> Who plans to leave you for the beckoning west,
> You tear apart your softly clinging veils,
> And hold him captive by your loveliness,
> Enraptured this, he cannot leave your side;
> Careless to know his golden chariot waits
> So he can touch you with his burning lips
> And watch the mantling crimson of sweet shame
> Grow deeper with each new caress,
> And though, perforce, he leaves you at the last,
> He turns again, with laughter and a sigh,
> To kiss the nipples of your naked breasts
> And so is gone! (p. 73).

Had Morton stayed in her birthplace of Limerick such sensuality in her writing might have brought her into conflict with the Irish Censorship Board although, at that time, poetry was not censored as severely as prose. Living and working in Belfast gave her the freedom to explore her own aesthetic.

Four collections of her poetry were published in her lifetime. Her *Masque in Maytime* (1948) is a long poem about the dance of trees personified as women who wake up in spring and grow to maturity before being assaulted violently by a hailstorm. Morton herself described it, in the prelims of her pamphlet, as:

> an experimental work. In it the author has tried, by the use of a variety of metres, to capture the colour and rhythm, the accompanying music and the underlying theme of a natural ballet produced on an Ulster landscape by the caprice of the Ulster climate.

Kirkland observed that this poem, too, has a sexual undercurrent with a crescendo in a dance that mimics orgasm but even he does not state the obvious – *Masque in Maytime* is about the rape of women by men:

> Fleeting maidens, backward glancing,
> Ice-shod demons, madly prancing,
> Stinging lashes, icy whips,
> Barren kisses, frozen lips,
> Demons leaping,
> Maidens weeping,
> Twisting, turning, stooping, spurning,
> Striving with a frenzied grace
> To evade that cold embrace.
> (*Masque in Maytime*, 1948, np)

It is worth noting that, at the conclusion of the poem, it is the figure of Pity and not Justice that arrives to comfort the devastated women. Were Morton writing *Masque in May* today it is likely that her critique of male violence would be more trenchant.

In her first collection a poem titled *Retrospect* displays a feistiness of spirit that she develops in later work:

> I know you loved me;
>   Although your words were cold,
>   Your voice the secret told:
>   Vain words, by love controlled,
>   Dear voice, by love made bold:
>   Across a grief grown old
>   I write in gleaming gold
> I know you loved me (p. 79).

A Harsh Environment

May Morton was born in Limerick in the later nineteenth century, though there is some confusion about the actual year of her birth. *The Field Day Anthology of Irish Writing: Volume IV* gives it as 1876. According to the National Census of 1901 she was aged twenty-two in 1901 and living in County Tyrone. For the purposes of this anthology I am using the census figure of 1879 as the likely year of her birth. Coming from a Protestant background, she moved to the north and got a job as a teacher in the Belfast Model School for Girls where she subsequently became vice-principal. In her last collection, *Sung to a Spinning Wheel*, the poem titled *Dedication to a Teacher* begins with a stanza indicating her view on the role of a teacher:

> Let me be strong that little children may
> Grow confident in living, day by day:
> Nor let my strength supplant their own,
> They stand erect who learn to stand alone.

Hers was a liberal view that did not chime with the times. The Irish Free State was monocultural, religiously conservative and rigidly inward-looking. The new Northern Ireland state had been constructed to protect the Unionist majority. At its beginning Northern Ireland was a place in which sectarianism and internecine conflict was endemic. The Ulster Unionist Party was in government for the next fifty years during which time the nationalist population suffered discrimination. In the south of Ireland, too, this was a period of political retrenchment in the aftermath of the revolutionary period (1916–2023). The 1916 leader James Connolly had forecast that the imposition of partition on the island of Ireland would lead to "a carnival of reaction both North and South."[2] His prophetic view was borne out by John McGahern's subsequent assessment of Ireland in the 30s, 40s and 50s as "a society that was often bigoted, intolerant, cowardly, philistine and spiritually crippled."[3]

Once partition and independence had been achieved, women in Ireland, north and south, were swiftly relegated by law and custom, to the margins of economic, social and cultural life. It was a harsh environment for any woman whose ambition extended beyond the kitchen sink. During those years many women writers did continue to write and to have their work published, but it is only since the second wave feminist movement opened the way for literary feminism and for feminist reclamation work that, in many cases, their contribution to the cultural life of those times has begun to get the attention it deserves. May Morton is a case in point: her role in the second poetic revival[4] of the twentieth century in Northern Ireland was significant. Her participation was central to a number of literary associations that she helped to establish in Belfast. During her lifetime Morton's award-winning poetry was critically acclaimed and yet, until recently, both she and her work have been largely overlooked.

Spindle and Shuttle

Writing and publishing the long poem *Spindle and Shuttle* (1951) is Morton's greatest creative achievement. In this two-hundred line poem, she explores the lives of workers in the linen industry in Northern Ireland. It begins with a domestic image:

> Last night I darned a damask tablecloth.
>
> >Back and forth
> >Warp and woof.
>
> The cloth was old; a hundred years and more
> Had come and gone since, master of his loom,
> Some skilful weaver set the hare and hounds
> Careering through the woodland of its edge
> In incandescent pattern, white on white.
> It was my mother's cloth, her mother's too
> (Some things wear better than their owners do)
> And linen lasts: a stuff for shirts and shrouds
> Since Egypt's kings first built their gorgeous tombs
> And wrapped their dead in linen, it may be
> They held it symbol of a latent hope
> Of immortality.
> (*Pillars of the House*, 1987, 90)

The contrast between the homely image of the tablecloth and the masculine authority of ancient Egypt is deliberate. The poem celebrates the history of linen making in Ulster but, more importantly, it celebrates the role of *women* in that history. It moves from the cottage industry into nineteenth century capitalism, mechanisation of the mill and its attendant urbanisation:

> And women hurry, shapeless in their shawls,
> In multitudes made nameless, to the mill,
> Some young, some old, and many great with child:
> All wage slaves of the new industrial age, (92)

Yet again, there is a juxtaposition of female experience and male supremacy in this description of the "millies" heading to work while the "linen lords/build fine town mansions for their families." The poem does not wallow in nostalgia for rural life although Morton's affection for the countryside is evident. A flower is "As shy and secret as an Ulster maid/Who saves her smiles like shillings unaware/Life pays no dividends on thrifty love." Over time, there is progress towards a better life for workers. By the middle of the twentieth century the exploitation of the working class had been ameliorated and the stanzas develop a triumphant tone:

> The spinner and the weaver in the mill
> Now earn a living and have time to live,
> Children whose mothers were half-timers once
> Untouchables in factory and school
> May learn to play and even play to learn
> And think of spindle as a word to spell.
> Mill-girls have shed their shawl-cocoons and shine
> Brighter than butterflies (92/93).

At the end of the poem Morton expresses a concern shared by many poets of the post-war period of a potential apocalypse caused by the atomic bomb:

> Hear the clatter of the loom
> Atom bomb and day of doom!
> Will the clatter never cease?
> Work for war and hope for peace.
> Hear the spindle's gentler hum:
> Work for peace and peace may come (94).

A Late Flowering
In 1951 Morton's great poem, *Spindle and Shuttle,* won the prestigious Festival of Britain, Northern Ireland Poetry award. The poet was seventy-two years old when she

received her prize of a hundred pounds (valued at £3600 sterling today). Morton had come late to her craft. It was only after her retirement from teaching in the 1930s that, then in her mid-fifties, she felt free to write poetry in earnest. In just over twenty years she grew to become an eminent poet in Northern Ireland. The impression is of an artist who, in middle age, consciously shed the conventions of the times to pursue her own freedom of expression. A lifetime is condensed into the poetry of two decades: from youthful passion and belief in God in her early work, to the political and historical maturity of *Spindle and Shuttle* and ending, finally, with the meditativeness at work in her late poem *The Rope* which was published in *Sung to the Spinning Wheel* in 1952:

John & Roberta Hewitt, May Morton, PEN conference, Vienna, 1955

A phantom rope, a shadow on the gray,
moored fast to nothingness. The sullen sea,
secret, fog-burdened, with a pledge for me:
somewhere a ship, somewhere a landing lay.
A sea-bird's crying in a shrouded bay,
a soul's voice tearing at the mystery

of all that was and all that was to be,
what sun, what storm, what blue of summer day!

Veiled source, veiled destiny. Yet taut the span
of twisted cable where the life of man
binds each to each. The hand that made the rope
made a creator and a hope:
God-man, man-God, an endless unity
the ship, the rope, the landing and the sea (p 55).

Sung to a Spinning Wheel, Morton's final collection, traces her development as a poet. While returning often to her favoured theme of the natural world she also traces the reality of World War Two as experienced in Belfast. In *Blitzed*, she writes:

All down our street
where houses have no eyes;
bereft of sight,
with hands outstretched as in a cave
I grope for light.

In the late poems her concentration shifts from love to death as in *Milestone*:

Seed-time and harvest of the spirit's year:
Is this the cycle? Is the ending here?
Or, having slept, do souls awake once more
to live and love and labour as before.
If there be fresh adventure I'll find zest,
if sleep be all, I am content to rest.

Coffee culture, Biscuit chat.[5]
During her life, May Morton was a powerhouse of activism. She deserves to be remembered not only for her poetry, but for her commitment to developing international relations through the Belfast PEN Centre. In

her essay in *The Writer and The PEN* she outlined her philosophy:

> People sometimes ask what possible connection can there be between an author's work and the cause of international goodwill. It seems to me that the connecting link is the sincerity of the writer, for every misconception that is removed helps to make the way clear to further understanding, and understanding is the better part of charity. The writer, as such, has no power to adjust frontiers or to reform economic systems. It is his privilege to hold up a lamp … Infinite charity, absolute truth, these are the ideals that lie beyond our present horizon. But the PEN goal is progressive rather than static […] (1942, 2).

She was deeply involved in a number of literary organisations and journals. In 1946 she edited a collection of poetry, *Fleet of Dreams*, by Blanche Desmond Clyne, a young poet who died at the age of twenty. A founder member of the Young Ulster Society, Morton became secretary and subsequent chair of the Belfast Centre of PEN and a delegate to many PEN International conferences. She was part of a coterie of writers who had a significant impact on Northern Irish literature at the time. In a collection of essays in *The Oxford Handbook of Modern Irish Poetry* (2012) Richard Kirkland writes about the second northern poetic revival in his essay 'The Poetics of Partition: Poetry and Northern Ireland in the 1940s'. Its onset coincided with the beginning of the Second World War, or what the Queen's University of Belfast magazine, *The New Northman*, called "the present eruption of Nazi frightfulness," and was championed most energetically by the young student poet and critic Robert Greacen. Other significant poets involved were Roy McFadden and John Gallen, and, in a slightly more semi-detached way, John Hewitt, May Morton and W.R. Rodgers. It was a period of obsessive coterie building, anthology compiling and manifesto drafting, and had, according to Greacen, "an exhilarating tang, which led to perhaps more good work that might have been expected in the circumstances." Described by contemporary writer John Boyd as "poets and conversationalists," Greacen and McFadden (along with Gallen) "vigorously eschewed the weight of convention in preference for exuberant, romantic avant-garde self-examination." (*Poetics of Partition*, 2012, 211).

As can be seen from the line-up of writers, the second Northern poetic revival was predominately a male affair. Along with the aforementioned writers, Denis Ireland (essayist), William Conor (painter), Sam Hanna Bell, Joe Tomelty and Jimmy Vitty (librarian at the Linen Hall Library), attended frequently. Even Louis McNeice made the occasional appearance. While May Morton, along with Freda Laughton and Celia Randall, was one of only a handful of women who participated in the group that met in Campbell's Coffee House, opposite City Hall on Donegal Square West during the late 1930s and through the 1940s, she tends to be the one who gets a mention. Greacen stated that the conversation was "crisp, wryly humourous in the throwaway Northern fashion. It tends towards practicality rather than abstraction" (p. 219).

The Belfast PEN Centre
"It is not easy," May Morton wrote in relation to her PEN commitments, "to keep a liberal non sectarian society alive." (*Irish Women Poets Rediscovered*, 2021, p. 81). Yet she persisted, organising the Belfast Centre activities until the end of her life. In a letter to her Dublin-based friend Kathleen O'Brennan in 1945 she complained about the impossibility of holding meetings between the Northern and Southern centres while thanking the Dublin president

Maurice Walsh for his "kindly interest and understanding of our wish for a united Ireland PEN" (p. 81). Reading the papers of the Dublin PEN Centre of the time, I can appreciate her frustration. The focus of the Dublin Centre was on social events, garden parties and discussions that were rather grandly called *"conversaziones."* PEN Dublin Centre attracted an illustrious group of writers including Sean O'Faoláin, Norah Hoult, Bulmer Hobson, Lord Longford, Austin Clarke and later, Mary Lavin. In 1937 the writer Maurice Walsh invested time and effort into setting up the Belfast Centre under the presidency of Richard Rowley, with Morton as secretary. Members of Belfast PEN attended functions in Dublin although it seems to have been a largely one-way traffic. It was recorded in the minutes of the Dublin Centre that a return invitation to attend an event in Belfast in 1948 was not accepted as none of the board members were available to travel. A note in the minutes of the meeting of April 1951 could be read as being less than enthusiastic about the North/South link. "As Sean MacBride, Minister for External Affairs could not now come the guest of honour for dinner will be Patricia O'Connor, Chairman of the Belfast Centre."

It is no surprise that, in the male-dominated literary café-society of the 1940s in Belfast, Morton's contribution was under-appreciated. In his essay on May Morton, Stephen O'Neill wrote in *Irish Women Poets Rediscovered* that she was:

> Remembered somewhat disparagingly in 1979 by Roy MacFadden as a woman whose presence was felt at PEN meetings — 'whose gentle gloves sheathed knuckle dusters and for whom young poets were slight challenges in plasticine' — Morton seemed to cut an often-frustrated figure at these events. In the same piece, McFadden also memorably described her as 'Maud Gonne of the Ulster Union Club, Lady Gregory of PEN,' suggesting at once her importance in these

organisations but also her incongruity within the social and political confines of each organisation (2021, 81).

In her last poetry collection, *Sung to the Spinning Wheel*, Morton dedicates one poem to "The Author of *Flowers for a Lady*", the title of a poetry collection by Roy McFadden. Her poem begins:

> So tender are the pale blooms of your song,
> petal and leaf
> twined by a poet's grief,
> I turn each page with gentle reverent hands
> trying to understand
> how life may be a crucible of pain

She might have been less generous in her praise had she known what McFadden really thought of her. Even her good friend, the poet John Hewitt, could be condescending. In his poem *Roll Call* (written in 1942 and published in *Lagan*) he writes at length about the male members of the group but simply depicts May Morton as:

> That fine woman with the gentle skill
> For roses, words and friendship most of all (219).

In 1951, May Morton showed her true mettle as a poet and entered her poem *Spindle and Shuttle* for consideration for the Festival of Britain Northern Ireland poetry prize. It was held, that year, at the arts festival in Castlereagh. The subject was "Northern Ireland". She chose to write about the linen industry which had a central role in the economic life of Ulster and she focussed, specifically, on the lives of women working in that industry.

> All wage slaves of the new industrial age
> All temple vestals of the linen god.
> (*Pillars of the House*, 1987, 92).

The two judges, W.R. Rodgers and H.O. White, selected her poem over hundreds of others. In the face of competition from a poem as celebrated as John Hewitt's *The Colony*, which he had submitted to the same competition, her win was an extraordinary achievement. Hewitt's poem is a study on the impact of the Ulster Plantation and, according to Stephen O'Neill, it is "regionalist and essentially masculine apologia" (*Irish Women Rediscovered*, 77). John Hewitt was a prolific and influential Northern Irish writer who became so admired that he acquired the soubriquet of Ulster's Poet Laureate. By contrast, May Morton's poem is about the experiences of ordinary working women. It is written in a rich and inventive way. Her use of a refrain to echo the movement of the shuttle gives the poem a textured weave:

> Back and forth
> Warp and woof
> Wing of angel
> Devil's hoof (92).

Spindle and Shuttle was selected as the winner by the judges who determined that: "The poem has remarkable qualities, it is original in design, it is a sustained effort and it breathes the spirit of our Province" (Festival Committee, *Northern Ireland Prize Poems*, 1951, np). At one point the poet is critiquing capitalism while, at the same time, she maintains the rhythm of the shuttle, thus giving the poem a dreamlike quality:

> Darning, dreaming,
> Thinking long,
> Flax and flux and wheel and song;
> Good and evil,
> Right from wrong.
>
> Spend and lend and buy and borrow,
> Yesterday, to-day, to-morrow;
> Weaving linen,
> Spinning thread,
> Weaving guns and spinning bread;

Sheets and shrouds
And shirts and collars
Earning dollars, dollars, dollars! (93)

The Hallmark of Truth

There seems to be no record of May Morton's response to the granting of this prize but it is easy to imagine her sense of vindication. Such affirmation of her work could not be ignored by the male literati dominating the Belfast scene of the time. Unusually, the judges decided to award an additional prize that year. Yet again, the award went to a woman, Phyllis Gailey, whose previous published poetry was described rather dismissively as "lighthearted." There was nothing light-hearted about May Morton's life nor her work. Her commitment to her art was unflinching. While she resisted the patriarchal culture of the time, she found it impossible to fully realise an alternative model in which a woman's imagination could flourish. According to Jaclyn Allen:

> While Morton is able to articulate that the model of feminine creativity needs to change and gestures towards a way forward, the model remains in liminal space and does not materialise within the self or within the external world, indicating difficulty in enacting this change (*A History of Irish Women's Poetry*, 2021, p. 195).

Despite the odds, Morton left her mark in significant ways. She wrote poems about the experience of being a woman that moved beyond the "spiritually crippled times" that she was living in. She worked hard to build international connections through literature. Most importantly, her dedication to the truth was unswerving. It was an imperative, she wrote, the writer has an obligation to tell the truth:

> Let the Ulster writer paint the Ulster background with fidelity, whether it be farm or factory, the glory of a gorse-crowned hill or the squalor of a city slum ... Any work of art should bear the imprint of its creator's personality. But it should also bear the hallmarks of Truth. Sincerity is all (*The PEN in Ulster*, 1942, p. 1).

Morton's advice to writers "to bear the hallmarks of Truth" epitomises the *raison d'étre* of the organisation to which she dedicated so much of her life. The Charter of PEN International organisation describes its fundamental purpose in Section 4:

> PEN stands for the principle of unhampered transmission of thought within each nation and between all nations, and members pledge themselves to oppose any form of suppression of freedom of expression in the country and community to which they belong, as well as throughout the world wherever this is possible. PEN declares for a free press and opposes arbitrary censorship in time of peace. It believes that the necessary advance of the world towards a more highly organised political and economic order renders a free criticism of governments, administrations and institutions imperative. And since freedom implies voluntary restraint, members pledge themselves to oppose such evils of a free press as mendacious publications, deliberate falsehood and distortion of facts for political and personal ends (*PEN Illustrated 100 Years*, 2022, p. 300).

During her lifetime, May Morton strived, and failed to bring about a "united Ireland PEN." Today her ambition has been realised: Irish PEN/PEN na hÉireann is a single all-Ireland entity. It draws its members from both jurisdictions on the island. The Irish Centre is one of PEN International's global network of one hundred and forty-five centres in five continents. As well as working in developed democracies, PEN International operates in many countries, including Myanmar, China and Afghanistan, where the systems of government are inimical to the principle of freedom of expression.

Conclusion

May Morton died in 1957. During her lifetime, the constraints on writers living on the island of Ireland were stark. By 1935 the Register of Prohibited Publications showed six hundred and eighteen books in total were banned in Ireland. In 1942 Sir John Keane told the Irish Senate (Seanad Éireann) that sixteen hundred books had been banned since independence. By 1967 the number had reached almost ten thousand books. Today, virtually all banned books in Ireland have been unbanned. In Northern Ireland, a less comprehensive Roman Index of Censorship applied to Catholics and the Unionist-dominated state was deeply suspicious of intellectual thought and exploration. These conditions created a society within which May Morton found it difficult to keep alive a liberal, non-sectarian literary organisation that promoted freedom of expression as a universal right. It is to Morton's credit that she persisted in championing that cause to the end of her life.

After her death May Morton's works of poetry were eclipsed by the contributions of poets of that time, including John Hewitt and Roy McFadden. She had no descendents to keep her memory alive. Apart from the publication of *Spindle and Shuttle* in the collection *Pillars of the House* (Wolfhound Press, 1987), the first reclamation anthology of Irish women's poetry, her life and work has been largely forgotten. Thankfully, after years of neglect, there has been some revival of academic interest in Morton's poetry, as Jaclyn Allen and Stephen O'Neill's works attest.

Today, Ireland, both in north and south, is a more open and liberal society where freedom of expression is celebrated. In many other parts of the world, the writer faces persecution. PEN International has a global reach and supports hundreds of writers who are being punished for daring to exercise that freedom. It is a sobering thought that, regardless of the circumstances, there will always be writers brave enough to use their creative talents in the fight against oppression. As Lucie Aubrac, the French resistance writer, has said: "le verbe 'résister' existe depuis que les étres humains sont capable de refléchir."[6] (*La Résistance expliquée á mes petits-enfants*, Edition du Seuil, 9).

In many parts of the world, the writer is censored, criminalised, tortured or even condemned to death. May Morton's efforts to keep the Belfast PEN Centre alive were an expression of her deeply felt conviction that, for literature's sake, a writer must be free to write the truth. It was a view that she expressed with passion, when she wrote:

> Any work of art should bear the imprint of its creator's personality. But it should also bear the hallmarks of Truth. Sincerity is all.

NOTES

1. PEN is an international literary organisation in which Morton was active. Its motto is 'Literature knows no Frontiers.' *The PEN in Ulster* (1942) was the first publication of essays by members of the PEN Belfast Centre. Morton wrote the introductory essay.
2. *Labour in Irish History* 1904.
3. Quoted in Colm Toibin's *Walking along the Border* (1988 87).
4. In *The Poetics of Partition* (2012), Richard Kirkland describes the two other revivals as, "The first, in the early years of the century, existed as part of a cultural revival more usually characterized as concentrated in drama and performance ... the third revival is usually identified as emerging during the mid to late 60s with Belfast as its hub.'

5   From McFadden's poem *Coffee at Crumbles* (1979).
6   Trans: The verb 'to resist' has existed for as long as humans have been capable of thinking.

May Morton:
Phantom Poet

Dawn and Afterglow
(Belfast, The Quota Press, 1936)

Dawn

Dawn

Dawn came clad in sunshine,
   Shod with rosy light,
Kissing all the hill-tops
   In her blithesome flight;
Shadows fled before her,
   Bright streams gleamed and glances,
Dark wood waked to music
   As her light limbs danced.
Knowing naught of sorrow,
   Innocent of wrong,
Life (she thought) is laughter,
   Love (she sighed) is song!

If I Had a Lover

If I had a lover I'd want him to see
That slender young moon on a branch of a tree!

If I had a lover, on tip-toe we'd go
Along where the river runs silent and slow.

If I had a lover 'twould be my delight
To show him two moons on the very same night.

If I had a lover (so foolish am I)
I'd give him the slender young moon from the sky!

A SLENDER YOUNG MOON ON THE BRANCH OF A TREE

The Oak, He is a Farming Man

The oak, he is a farming man,
   With hands all gnarled with toil,
Whose folks for generations have
   Been rooted to the soil.

The beech, she is the farmer's wife,
   Who wears a spreading gown
To make her look important when
   She's going up to town.

The pine, he is a wicked monk
   Who hides within his hood,
And hopes that all his brother monks
   Will think him wise and good.

The birch, she is a dainty maid
   So slender and so tall,
All dressed in shining silver, like
   A princess at a ball.

The larch, he is an Ulsterman
   That's sturdy, straight, and true,
And makes me think of somebody
   Well! – somebody like you.

WEEPING DOWN THE MOUNTAIN WAY

Mountain Mist

Maiden of the mountain mist,
Stooping boldly to be kissed
When the young and ardent sun
First pursues you – half in fun,
Wherefore snatch your robe of grey
From his grasp, and haste away
When his passion's hot desire
Follows you with lips of fire?

Foolish maiden, hiding there
In the blue and silent air,
Know that love lives but a day,
Even now he flies away.

Lonely maid, at close of day,
Weeping down the mountain way,
Love has gone and left but this –
Memory of a morning kiss.

My Pal

I found a little donkey
    In a lane in Donegal,
A poor wee bare-foot donkey
    Without any shoes at all.

His hoofs were very tiny,
    And the lane was very wet,
So I took him to the smithy
    To be fitted with a set.

I clipped him and I combed him,
    I fattened him with corn,
And called him "Saint Columba"
    For the place where he was born.

He's stupid and he's lazy
    He's as crabbed as can be,
And a town life doesn't suit him;
    But he's just the pal for me.

So when things get quite beyond me,
    And I can't get on at all,
I go off with Saint Columba
    Through the lanes of Donegal.

Boat Song

Good comrades, when
    Will you sail again
For the misty Hebrides,
    Where the sea-bird cries,
    And the salt spray flies
In the freshening western breeze?

To watch once more
    Along Skavaig's shore
The leap and crash of a wave,
    And to strain and street
    While you hide your fear
That you'll find a viking's grave!

To drift at will
    When the winds are still,
And to lie in Broadford Bay
    As the sun sinks low,
    And the Coolins glow
To the farewell kiss of day.

The songs we'll sing,
    And the thoughts we'll bring
To our talk of life and love,
    Through the long twilight
    Of the northern light,
With the clear pale sky above.

So, comrades, when
    Will you sail again ?
Let the day come swift and soon
    For a land life palls
    When the bright wave calls
On a breezy morn in June!

Snowdrops

'Tis winter in my garden now and everything looks bare,
Harsh, biting winds are telling me that snow is in the air,
But soon the joyous blackbird will trill forth his song of glee,
For I see the snowdrops peeping – round the tree.

I know that in the summer-time the garden will be gay
With roses and anemones, with lavender and may,
I love their fragrant beauty, but they're not so dear to me
As the fragile little snowdrops round the tree.

Like faithful friends, who banish grief with loving words that cheer,
These gallant little flowerets break the sadness of the year;
Oh! February's fair maids, you are sweet and pure to see
In your white and dainty dresses, round the tree.

Favourites

1

I thought that the nicest walk under the sun
Was up by Glen Ann and back home by Glen Dun,
Until I discovered a much better plan
Was to go up Glen Dun and come back by Glen Ann.

2

Now, when I stay at Cushendall,
I never settle there at all,
For, willy-nilly, I must run
Across the hill to Cushendun,

But, when I stay at Cushendun,
It's just the same – away I run ,
It seems I'm hardly there at all
Till off I go to Cushendall!

Afterglow

Evening lay in the valley
Watching the afterglow
Lighting the great white mountains,
Tinting the virgin snow:
Joyous and fair as the dawning,
Rosy as love's delight,
How could she know
That the afterglow
Is the prelude to the night!

Recompense

Lilting and joyous as the linnet's song
My simple strains; till, envying love's content,
Death smote the strings. Stricken, its joy all spent,
Its music hushed, love suffered yet no wrong,
Folded in silence and by tears made strong,
As hidden seed to winter's grieving lent,
Will swell and struggle till the sheath be rent
That holds it prisoned and confined too long.

Fruitful the love you gave me long ago:
In my heart's dark deep-sown, it flowers again;
Nurtured so well, from its excess must flow
Such gentle healing for another's pain,
Such store of comfort for another's woe,
That through death love shall live, and grief be gain.

Divided

Over the heather we walked,
we two together,
Golden the level sun shone, gold on the purple.

Out of the silence, I cried,
cried to my lover,
"Something has plundered our hearts, leaving them empty."

Only the echoes replied
"Empty - - - empty."
Over the heather we walked, brooding and lonely.

Aftermath

Farewell!
You leave me, love, too soon,
Though quenched your thirst:
Your eyes are cold and do not seek for mine
As at the first.

'Twas but last night your love you swore,
While I, thought silent, loved the more.

Sweet soft caresses
Of gentle hands, and lips that clung
In kisses that were hid among
My loosened tresses:
Till, all on fire,
Our separate beings mingled and distilled
Within one sparkling, crystal goblet, filled
To our desire.

Farewell!
And should you come agaiun
To quench your thirst,
No more, for you, the fountain shall be clear
As at the first.

'Twas but last night your love you swore,
While I, though silent, loved the more.

A Thought

Fragments of beauty,
    Petal and flower,
Bird-song and starlight,
    Live but an hour.

Part of God's garden,
    Planted as we:
How can you know "was, "
    "is", or "to be"?

The Hidden Scroll

In all things unity,
Completeness:
Day's burning kiss brings to the languid earth
The earth's cool breath,
Spring, straining at the womb, must yet await
The winter's death;
The helmsman steers his ship to anchorage,
Each winged seed
Torn from its fragile stem by winter's rage
Finds earth at need.

In all things harmony,
Fulfilment:
Ever, love-summoned by the primal call
Of man's desire,
Come yielding lips that seek for his, and hold
An answering fire;
Yet knows his frustrate soul nor destiny,
Nor source, nor goal,
Though reason strive, and blindfold faith, to read
The hidden scroll.

I Met a Friend

"I met a friend", we lightly say,
   And go as lightly on our way,
On coming pleasures still intent
   – For that is how our youth is spent.

"I met a friend", we smiling say,
   And stay to greet him by the way,
Tell what we did and where we went
   – And that's how middle life is spent.

"I met a friend", we, thankful, say,
   When lonely grows the quiet way,
For hearts may glow though backs are bent
   – Ah! that is how old age is spent.

"I met a friend" , so shall we say
   When at the ending of the way
We lay our weary limbs to rest,
   And death says gently "This is best".

LANGUID FERNS WITH LONG GREEN FINGERS

To Glenariff

Let gentle darkness fold you in her cloak, beloved glen,
Till grey-winged dawn shall summon you to keep our
 tryst again.
Creative light shall draw you, pale and wan, from night's
 caress,
And paint afresh the radiant hues that grace your
 loveliness:
Enchanted day shall pause in ecstasy till you awake
To hear the first sweet chorus of the woods dim silence
 break:
The mournful hills shall raise their drooping veils, and
 cease to weep,
Their griefs all gathered to your ravaged heart and hidden
 deep:
Dark, crowding pines shall step from out the mist with
 soundless tread,
And stand aloof in brooding watchfulness when mists
 have fled:
The sun shall softly throw upon your couch his golden
 spears,
And kiss your heavy eyelids, shadowed with the
 mountain's tears,
Until you smile: while wood-anemones so frail and fair
Embroider with their stars of glowing white the robe you
 wear.
And I shall hear your laughter where the stream runs swift
 and clear,
And feel your fragrant breath upon my cheek, your soul so
 near
That it shall stoop on shining wings to bless some quiet
 pool
Where languid ferns with long green fingers touch the
 waters cool
While its pure flame, enshrined in solitude, remote, divine,

Shall merge its whiteness in the redder glow that burns in mine.

Then I will lend you to the world once more, since that must be,
But in this sacred hour you still shall keep your soul for me.

Exiled

I never see a tall cliff rise
Between the wave and sky,
I never watch the sea-birds dive,
Nor hear their hungry cry,
But I would be a child once more
To play beside the Antrim shore
And see the ships go by.

I never listen to the sound
Of any mountain rill,
Nor smell the perfume of the whins
That grow on any hill,
But I would be a boy again
To wander through an Antrim glen,
And fish the streamlets still.

I never see the silver light
That shines on any bay,
Nor heard the singing of a lark
On any summer's day,
But I could wish that I had stayed
To wed the smiling Antrim maid
I kissed one morn in May!

Lament of the Keening Women – Arranmore

Sad priestesses of dark, despairing woe,
In trailing shawls of black the women go,
Thro' mists that cannot hush the wailing cry
That lifts its bitter clamour to the sky
Or trembles to a moaning low and deep
In ecstasy of grief that may not weep;
From isle to isle the mournful chanting rolls
"Oh, God! Have pity on their sinful souls!

Oh, Saviour who upon the cross has bled,
Command the sea to give us back our dead:
Mother of sorrows, ours the pain you bore,
Pray for their souls. They will return no more,
They will return no more!

Our sons are dead, the beautiful, the brave,
They cried, oh God ! but there was none to save:
Our arms are empty, desolate our shore,
Our sons are dead. They will return no more,
They will return no more!

Isle of Mist

1

Weave, fair enchantress of the northern seas,
Your endless-seeming webs of witchery:
Weave fire and mist and cloudy gossamer
In faery robes of ever-changing light;
So shall your raiment still befit your mood,
And sameness never dull your beauty's lure.

So pure you seem when, garbed in fairest white,
You stand beneath the jewelled dome of heaven,
Remote and cold as barren chastity:
So modest, in the gown of sober grey
You don with such a penitential air
To sadden morning with your constant tears:
So gentle, when about your form you draw
A mantle of the calm and holy blue
Which makes the noon-day sky look wan and pale,
And steals the sapphire from the envious sea.

2

Soft, now, the June night calls: and sea and sky
Shall know you for the wanton that you are!

Enamoured of your fiery parapmour
Who plans to leave you for the beckoning west,
You tear apart your coftly clinging veils,
And hold him captive by your loveliness.
Enraptured thus, he cannot leave your side;
Careless to know his golden chariot waits
So he can touch you with his burning lips
And watch the mantling crimson of sweet shame
Grow ever deeper with each new caress.

And though, perforce, he leaves you at the last
He turns again, with laughter and a sigh,
To kiss the nipples of your naked breasts,
And so is gone!
Sleep fair enchantress, sleep
Beneath your coverlet of purpling dark,
Content to know that he must come again:
For that same parting kiss that sealed you his
Has fettered him, he is love's prisoner, too,
And cannot choose but come to you again.

Shadows

My mind shall be my cinema to-night,
Switch off the light,
And memory shall throw upon the screen,
In mood serene,
The shadows of a thousand lovely things:

A sea-bird's wings –
Two slender arches in a stormy sky:
A butterfly
That hovers tremblingly above a rose:
Like flashing silver down the mountain-side:
An ebbing tide,
With gaudy sails upon a golden bay
At close of day:
A rosy granite peak enwreathed in mist,
By dawn new kissed:
The liquid crimson of the afterglow
On hills of snow:
The myriad stars that in the blue night sky
March, singing, by:
– Hold, memory! Hush! That anthem
of the spheres
My fancy hears.

Elusive strain! relentless in its flight –
Switch on the light.

Round my Garden

I'd hate to have a garden where everything just came
Out of a seedman's catalogue,
And bore a Latin name.

But here's a rose from Kathleen, and one from Cousin John,
And those are slips I grew myself,
See how they're coming on!

A bluebell from Glenariff, a primrose from Glen Dun,
A bit of gorse from Tiveragh
I planted – just for fun.

A juniper from Narin in County Donegal,
I had to coax it months and months
To make it root at all,

That lilac knows a secret that only two may share,
The beds are full of memories,
I sow them everywhere.

And, sometimes, when I'm lonely and no one comes to tea,
I ask my little garden friends
To tell their tales to me.

The Test

I will not ask you what you have,
   I care not greatly what you do,
But you must show me what you are
   Before I make a friend of you.

Retrospect

I know you loved me;
    Although your words were cold,
    Your voice the secret told:
    Vain words, by love controlled,
    Dear voice, by love made bold :
    Across a grief grown old
    I write in gleaming gold
I know you loved me.

TO STREW THE SCULPTURED LILIES ON THE LAKE

Whither?

When, through the bars of death, my curious eyes
The freed soul's habitation would behold,
Indifferent to a heaven with streets of gold,
And timorous of the far, unfriendly skies,
They seek a more familiar paradise
Upon the homely earth. Here, grown more bold,
They rest on well-loved hills, where clear and cold
The bright streams beckon, and the white mist flies.

To wake the celandine in woods long bare,
To strew the culptured lilies on the lake,
To bid the violets bend their heads in prayer,
To gild the willows for the children's sake,
My spirit's tasks. God made the flowers, and so
Perhaps his angels linger where they grow.

Masque in Maytime
(Lisburn, The Lisnagarvey Press, 1948)

Masque in Maytime

The stillness breathes as all the curtained dark
grows vibrant with a hushed expectancy;
the garden, sleeping in the shawl of night
stirs restlessly and sighs. But morning waits,
eager. Bright-sandalled, in the shadowy wings
till, with a startled and uneasy cry,
a lone bird twitters, sleeps, than cries again
with twitterings grown urgent "Wake! awake!"
and, as the chorus of bird music swells
to clear, full-throated ecstasy, the dawn
raises night's filmy curtains, one by one.
        Wake!
        Wake!
    Awake! awake! awake!
Joy, joy, joy! Let morning break, let morning break!
  Sing, sing, sing! Joyous morn, joyous morn!
  Joy, joy, joy! Day is born, day is born!
        Beauty!
        Beauty!
    Weep, weep, weep!
  Sing, sing, sing! Joyous morn, joyous morn!
  Joy, joy, joy! Day is born, day is born!
        Beauty!
        Beauty!
    Weep, weep, weep!
Sing, sing, sing! Let morning break, let morning break!
        Wake!
        Wake!
    Awake, awake, awake!

Responsive now the dancers of the dawn,
gay children of the Maytime, fair as love,
golden as happiness, glide nimbly forth
and fill the shadowed scene with radiant light.

                Shimmering,
                Glimmering,
        Out of the dawn
    Golden-limbed dancers flit over the lawn;
Waking the blossoming trees as they pass,
Lighting the dew-lamps a-swing in the grass:
                Shimmering,
                Glimmering,
        Radiant and fair,
Flinging their gossamer scarves in the air,
                Shimmering,
                Glimmering,
        Daring and gay,
Golden-limbed dancers leap into the sky!

In charming pose upon the tinselled lawn,
miming an interlude, the flowering trees
bow smiling recognition each to each:
a white-flounced cherry who till now has been
the prima ballerina of the stage
admires, though with a scarcely veiled dismay,
the glowing youth and careless artistry
of pyrus pirouetting on her toes:
a bride-plant in a pearl-embroidered gown
leans on the air her slender loveliness
and shyly hangs her head. Two apple trees
grown dignified and tall through many Mays
still wear with vanity their rich brocades:
a silver birch, wild dryad of the woods,
With stretching arms like green up-leaping flames,
partners a lilac whose demure appeal
is burdened by her heavy purple crown.
Laurels and hollies, aping armoured knights
Dark-visaged in their shining coats of mail,
Crowd in the wings and stand aloof and stern.

A hush, a pause, a conscious fluttering,
a sigh that ends the miming.
                       Now the dance!

Laughing breezes come and go,
      Come and go, come and go,
As the trees all curtsey low,
      Curstey low, curtsey low.
  Every breeze that comes to woo
  Is a lover fond and true:
  Every tree with blossomed bough
  Has become a maiden now!

Cherry wearing white and green
Swings her spreading crinoline
      As through minuet and tango,
      Slow pavane and swift fandango,
      Bright winds call and sunbeams say
      "Dance! Dance! merry, merry maids of May!"

Pyrus in a scarlet dress
Trembles at each light caress
      As through minuet and tango,
      Slow pavane and swift fandango,
      Bright winds call and sunbeams say
      "Dance! Dance! merry, merry maids of May!"

Bride-plant robed in pearly white
Swoons in transports of delight
      As through minuet and tango,
      Slow pavane and swift fandango,
      Bright winds call and sunbeams say
      "Dance! Dance! merry, merry maids of May !"

Silver birch so slim and fair
Flings her dainty limbs in air

  As through minuet and tango,
  Slow pavane and swift fandango,
  Bright winds call and sunbeams say
  "Dance! Dance! merry, merry maids of May!"

Lilac in a puple gown
Sways her flounces up and down
  As through minuet and tango,
  Slow pavane and swift fandango,
  Bright winds call and sunbeams say
  "Dance! Dance! merry, merry maids of May!"

Apples rather prim and staid
Rustle in their stiff brocade
  As through minuet and tango,
  Slow pavane and swift fandango,
  Bright winds call and sunbeams say
  "Dance! Dance! merry, merry maids of May!"

Pert azaleas in the grass
Kiss their partners when they pass
  As through minuet and tango,
  Slow pavane and swift fandango,
  Bright winds call and sunbeams say
  "Dance! Dance! merry, merry maids of May!"

  Faster, faster grows the measure,
  Life is rhythm and love is pleasure,
  Every dancer mad and merry –
  Lilac, pyrus, brideplant, cherry –
  Flirting, flaunting, swinging, swaying,
  All the world has gone a-maying!
  Whirling, twirling, gay, beguiling,
  Teasing, pleasing, sighing, smiling,
  Till at last the wild crescendo
  Fades to soft diminuendo,

      Spellbound maidens languid grow
      As the pale winds, sighing, go –
      All their lingering tenderness
      Gentle in a last caress.

Held in an ecstasy of golden dream
the trees, enchanted, stand. The amorous sun,
long fingers warm as quivering heart-strings stretched
from out life's burning core, now claims the morn
with benediction that is part embrace.
Light gathers the rare moment to enfold
its sweetest perfection in eternity.
Then all the beauty turns to melody
for loveliness is music whose clear voice
binds earth to heaven in one transcendent note
that vibrates and is gone.
                       A troubled breath,
half shadow and half sound, shatters the spell
that holds the shining day entranced in time.
The wind-strings moan till their discordant wail
creates the anguished fear they seek to still,
wild panic of unreason swells and spreads
as terror summons terror with a cry!
For all the listening trees are trembling now
with premonition of impending ill:
the cherry's white and supplicating hands
implore the heavens, the lilac bends to earth
fearful and shuddering. One by one pale forms
in frantic movements stoop and lean and strain,
as though by strategy each might escape
the sacrament of pain that all must share.

      Louder the wailing wind-strings call,
      Darker the swift cloud-shadows fall:
      Storm-demons armed with icy flail
      Leap to the earth in lashing hail!

Dancing! Prancing! Never maid
May escape the demons'raid:
Dancing! Prancing! Now they press,
Trampling on that loveliness.

Bride-plant, dishevelled in her pain,
Is beaten to the earth again!
    Fleeting maidens, backward glancing,
    Ice-shod demons, madly prancing,
     Stinging lashes, icy whips,
     Barren kisses, frozen lips,
      Demons leaping,
      Maidens weeping,
   Twisting, turning, stooping, spurning,
    Striving with a frenzied grace
    To evade that cold embrace.

Cherry, with writhings of distress,
Is prisoned in that wild caress!
    Fleeting maidens, backward glancing,
    Ice-shod demons, madly prancing,
     Stinging lashes, icy whips,
     Barren kisses, frozen lips,
      Demons leaping,
      Maidens weeping,
   Twisting, turning, stooping, spurning,
    Striving with a frenzied grace
    To evade that cold embrace.

Pyrus, in terror and alarm,
Must yield and lose her fair young charm!
    Fleeting maidens, backward glancing,
    Ice-shod demons, madly prancing,
     Stinging lashes, icy whips,
     Barren kisses, frozen lips,
      Demons leaping,

                    Maidens weeping,
          Twisting, turning, stooping, spurning,
                Striving with a frenzied grace
                To evade that cold embrace.

          Passion spent, the demons leave,
          Broken now, the maidens grieve,
          Sighing, sighing their despair,
          Weeping, weeping everywhere.

Dark, dark the gloom of sorrow's hour
Till, lovely as a new-blown flower,
In sudden radiance angel-bright
A wraith-like fantasy appears,
Her robe of many-coloured light
A web of sunbeams sewn with tears.
Above the misery and stress
She raises shining hands to bless,
Writes out her message on the air,
Smiles once, and is no longer there!

But gentle Pity, veiled in grey,
Healer and comforter, will stay
To share the maidens' bitter pain
And, weeping with them, will remain
To cleanse their grief of shames and fears
With her pure benizon of tears.

The masque is ended, and the music stilled
to fitful sighing. On the storm-drenched lawn
the mournful trees – frail puppets of the wind
who danced and mimed a life's vicissitudes –
caressed in sunshine and deflowered in hail
have crowned the rainbow with their grieving now
and stand quiescent in the healing rain.

Spindle and Shuttle
(Belfast, HM Stationery Office, 1951)

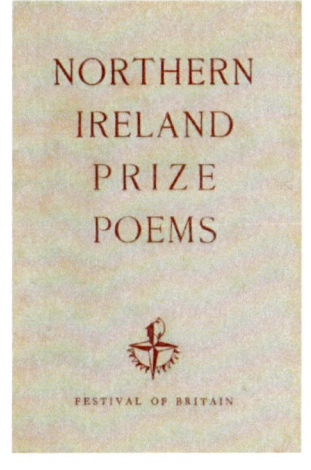

Spindle and Shuttle

Last night I darned a damask tablecloth.

      Back and forth
      Warp and woof.

The cloth was old; a hundred years and more
Had come and gone since, master of his loom,
Some skilful weaver set the hare and hounds
Careering through the woodland of its edge
In incandescent pattern, white on white.
It was my mother's cloth, her mother's too
(Some things wear better than their owners do)
And linen lasts: a stuff for shirts and shrouds
Since Egypt's kings first built their gorgeous tombs
And wrapped their dead in linen, it may be
They held it symbol of a latent hope
Of immortality.

      Back and forth
      Warp and woof:
      Wing of angel,
      Devil's hoof.

The glinting needle with its fitful spark,
My Jack o' Lantern on the marsh's dark,
Would pause and shine, would flash and flit along
Divining scene and symbol for a song.

A field of blossomed flax in North Tyrone
Its lean and sheen and shine, its small blue flower
As shy and secret as an Ulster maid
Who saves her smiles like shillings, unaware
Life pays no dividends on thrifty love.

Darning, learning
Yarning, yearning,
Spinning, weaving,
Joying, grieving:

A black flax dam, a field of linen snow,
Linked opposites: the scar upon the soul
Of every Ulsterman. (The spindle turns
And turning winds a thread where clumsy splice
Or stubborn knot will lie upon the spool
To mar the damask's smoothness when the web
Is woven fast).

Back and forth
Warp and woof:
Wing of angel,
Devil's hoof.

All times make time and all are good and ill;
Twin fibres twist to make the coiling rope
We label time.

                And good was twined with ill
When spinning yarn and weaving linen were
Still country crafts. The old blind woman with
Her spinning-wheel beside the open door
Would spin and spin with finger-tips for eyes
Matching the spindle's hunger to her own
Till each was satisfied; but she could feel
The warm sun on her face, the kindly wind
Lay gentle hands upon her faded hair.
The cottage weaver cramped and stiff from toil
That made a convict's treadmill of his loom
Could run a mile around his one green field
To flex his muscles; and could pause a while
To hear the blackbird's song, or sing his own

Back and forth
Warp and woof
Wing of angel
Devil's hoof:

The hand-loom turns to lumber and the wheel
Becomes a thing to win a tourist's glance
When far from field and bird the factories rise,
A myriad spindles and a maze of looms
Cradled within four walls. On every side
The streets of small brick houses spawn and sprawl
Though none could give its neighbour elbow-room.
Sleep flies each morning at the siren's shout
And women hurry, shapeless in their shawls,
In multitudes made nameless, to the mill,
Some young, some old, and many great with child:
All wage slaves of the new industrial age,
All temple vestals of the linen god.
Some will put off their shoes from off their feet
And barefoot serve the spindles all day long,
Some will keep constant vigil where the looms
Like giant nightmare spiders pounce and crawl
With spider skill across the tethered web
While captive shuttles darting to and fro
Will weave, not hare and hounds, but shamrock sprays
To tempt nostalgic exiles. None may rest
Till day ends and the siren sets them free.
Even the children, sad as wilting flowers
Plucked in the bud, must give their days to toil,
Their nights to weariness and never know
How morning comes with laughter to a child.
But linen prospers and the linen lords
Build fine town mansions for their families
And plan a city hall whose splendid dome
Will soar above the long lean streets and look
Beyond them to the green encircling hills.

Back and forth
Warp and woof:
Wing of angel
Devil's hoof:

Young men see visions and old men dream dreams:
Their beacons lit on summits far away,
Their faith entangled in the baffling rope,
Good twined with evil, evil twined with good.
Strand upon strand with whiter strands for some;
The spinner and the weaver in the mill
Now earn a living and have time to live,
Children whose mothers were half-timers once
Untouchables in factory and school
May learn to play and even play to learn
And think of spindle as a word to spell.
Mill-girls have shed their shawl-cocoons and shine
Brighter than butterflies. With gleaming hair
And ankles neat in nylon each can look
Into her mirror with a practised smile
And see herself the reigning linen queen.
The great domed hall four-square in stubborn stone
With polished marble floors magnificent
As any Rajah's palace has stood now
For nearly half a century. Strange how
The little laurel hedge that hems its lawns
Reveals we still are country-folk at heart
Deep-rooted in the fields our fathers tilled.

Back and forth
Warp and woof:
Wing of angel,
Devil's hoof:

The white strands catch the moment's light, and show
A pattern in the fabric, damask smooth.

We spin and weave, with yarns and years and tears
Our webs of linen and of destiny:
A people's life is netted in the loom
Their story echoes in the spindle's song.
Through slump to boom, through war to peace – this peace
The frightened hare with hounds upon her track
Running to meet the terror that she flees.

Darning, dreaming,
Thinking long,
Flax and flux and wheel and song;
Good and evil,
Right and wrong.

Spend and lend and buy and borrow,
Yesterday, to-day, to-morrow:
Weaving linen
Spinning thread
    Weaving guns and spinning bread;
Sheets and shrouds
And shirts and collars
    Earning dollars, dollars, dollars!

    See how fast the wheels are turning:
    Rome is burning, burning, burning!
Hear the crying of the fiddle:
Hands across and up the middle
Choose your partners for the dance
Weave your webs or take your chance!
Hear the clatter of the loom:
Atom bomb and day of doom!
Will the clatter never cease?
Work for war and hope for peace.
Hear the spindle's gentler hum:
Work for peace and peace may come.

In fields of North Tyrone, the bright flax grows,
The blackbird sings
And past the farm a quiet river flows.

Sung to the Spinning Wheel
(Belfast, Quota Press, 1952)

Sung to the Spinning Wheel

By MAY MORTON

May Morton
1952

1952
THE QUOTA PRESS,
2, MARCUS WARD STREET, BELFAST.

May Morton is a significant figure in contemporary Irish poetry, although her work is universal rather than regional or national in its appeal. She has contributed to "A Concord of Harps", the Irish P.E.N. Anthology, to many literary magazines and to B.B.C. programmes. A previous selection of her verse was published under the title "Dawn and Afterglow". Long poems which have been published in pamphlet form are "Masque in Maytime" and "Spindle and Shuttle" (which won the Festival of Britain, Northern Ireland, poetry award).

PRESS OPINIONS.

DAWN AND AFTERGLOW.

Whether the mood be joyous or sad beauty pervades all.
The Northern Whig.

A magical quality that traps the reader who discovers their delicate beauty.
Belfast Evening Telegraph.

MASQUE IN MAYTIME

The brief allegory is carried through with great vivacity and metrical skill to its quiet conclusion.
The Dublin Magazine.

SPINDLE AND SHUTTLE

The poem has remarkable qualities, it is original in design, it is a sustained effort and it breathes the spirit of our Province.
W. R. Rodgers and
Prof. H. O. White.

Singer-Spinner

Her foot on the treadle
her hand on the thread
a song in the wheel and a song in her head.

So busy, so busy the whirling without,
so urgent the clamour within:
the voice is a whisper, the whisper a shout
    "Let her spin!"
        "Let her sing!"
            "Let her spin!"

So many, so many the people without,
so lonely the person within:
the song full of discord, the singer in doubt
    "Let her spin!"
        "Let her sing!"
            "Let her spin!"

So faded, so faded the sunlight without,
so feeble the candle within:
The voice still a whisper, the whisper a shout
    "Let her spin!"
        "Let her sing!"
            "Let her spin!"

The Book

Between two covers of unchartered dark
               its strange leaves lie:
     close-written, line on line,
     your essay this – or mine,
            to live, to die.
And spendthrift youth may claim no extra page
nor one spare folio help penurious age.

Preposterous volume, where the writer is
           the reader too:
     scanning the story's trend
     the while he strives to bend
           the plot anew.
Scribbling his comments on the margin's white
painting fresh pictures for his soul's delight.

And, when the queer collaboration ends
           (for end it must
     as, equals once again,
     writer and brush and pen
           mingle their dust)
What of the book that must for ever be
upon the shelves of God's great library?

The Pearl

There was no benediction in your love
(A meteorite in my receptive earth
it lay within the wound – an alien thing).

There was no benediction in your love
nor any balm of bodies' unity;
ours was the fire that flint must strike from steel,
that which you had to give and I to take
seed of your soul to fill my soul's deep womb.
what could a woman do with such a gift
but sheathe it in her woman's tenderness,
and labour like an oyster in the dark
far down beneath the surface ebb and flow
till all the irk of conflict was resolved
and clothed upon with polished harmony.

Shall we have benediction at the last!
Not yours nor mine because both yours and mine;
your seed, my travail, ours the ripening yield –
the pearl of friendship for the hurt of love.

Street Tapestry

Backwards and forwards, round and round they go,
The trained car-beetles in their ballet show;
Their measured movements, so controlled, so free,
Weave and unroll a living tapestry
Where, prisoned in the fabric's warp and woof,
Nor drone nor worker dares to stand aloof.

A rhythmic pause! Bright shuttles glide between
The beaded jewels, crimson, gold and green.
Forward! Advance! Let individual skill
Complete the pattern of the human will,
Each whirling circle and concentric line
The slick perfection of evolved design.

*

If mathematics be the highest joy,
Creation the superb meccano toy
Of One who reckons not in terms of size,
Does God watch traffic with appraising eyes
That smile to see in men-machines as these
The geometric lore of ants and bees?

There are Three Things

There are three things a man has never done:
He has not killed a doctrine with a gun,
He has not planted weed and gathered corn,
Nor ever understood why he was born.

Women and Roses

Woman should grow in sweetness and disclose
a pilgrimage of beauty.
                                        Like the rose,
guarding her folded fragnance at the start,
learning to open wide her glowing heart
and share its tender loveliness with all
till, soundlessly, the perfumed petals fall,

Women and roses have so much to give
that only love can teach them how to live.

To M.E.T.B of Townley Hall

Her spirit dwelt in light, remote, serene,
  transcending strife,
and wove from tangled skeins of joy and pain
  harmonious life:
a rich, fair tapestry of shade on shade
  all subtly blent
with threads of gold to mark where shining love
  a radiance lent.

Dedication of a Teacher

Let me be strong that little children may
Grow confident in living, day by day:
Nor ever let my strength supplant their own,
They stand erect who learn to stand alone.

Let me be true that their young souls may shine
The brighter for the lamp that burns in mine
To help each part illuminate the whole
Where learning is the path and truth the goal.

Let me be just that they may learn from me
The gift to praise or blame impartially:
Let me be kind that they may understand
How mercy leads blind justice by the hand.

Let me be wise. Though knowledge be a tree
Where good and evil bloom in company,
From seeds of wisdom grafted on the bole
May spring the perfect flowering of the soul.

Ships

The midget ships, the restless, monstrous sea:
adventure now – and now security !
No night can hold an anchorage for all
so some must shorten sail and meet the squall
while others run before the wind and brag
they'll keep afloat and fly the pirate flag:
must they be wrecked, self-doomed by their belief
that seamanship can dodge the lodestar reef!

(Athwart the course that novices must steer
the Scylla and Charybdis of their fear).
With trembling compass, tossed by treacherous breeze,
the frail ships fight for freedom of the seas.

Moon-Spun

By moon-fire consecrate in mystic rite
my garden's incense fills the aisles of night:
   pale lilies crowd to worship there
   that each may bring a chalice rare
     brimful of light
drawn from the radiance of the shining flood
that sets a candle-flame in every bud.

The pale lawns glimmer with a burning dew
and, on the terrace, where once roses grew,
   frail, spectral vessels float and shine,
   bearing the moon-god's sacred wine
     to altars new
where every moonbeam is a vestal maid
who tends a shrine within some silvered shade.

The crystal walls of silence close around
that beauty's wistful soul, a refuge found,
   safe cloistered in the moon-spun dream
   that makes familiar places seem
     like holy ground,
may sing enchanted, soundless anthems there,
and build a temple on a wordless prayer.

Song of the Wild Bees
(from an old Gaelic song)

Gladsome the music of the wild bee's wings
On blossomed heather, where the warm air sings
For very joy on mountain and on brae
Till earth itself laughs with the shining day.

In all the world no music half so sweet
As this soft croon when bees and blossoms meet,
The murmuous chanting of their myriad wings,
Like faint harp-music played on elfin strings.

Give me a lonely hill, a summer sky
In whose blue depths nor cloud nor shadow lie,
The purpling heather all around me there
And wild bees crooning on the sunlit air.

Folk Songs from the Ukraine

The Gunner

Before I left my mother's knee
   The guns and shells were fun to me,
I played with them when other boys
   Were wasting time with foolish toys.

For I was a gunner from the start;
   I knew the use of every part
Before the vodka burnt my tongue,
   Or I could swear – and that was young!

As soon as I became a man
   I got a girl – a gunner can!
Last night I told her, half in fun,
   I loved her like I love my gun.

She has two plaits of coal-black hair
   As long as that gun's nozzle there,
Her eyes are stars that shine so clear
   They'd blind the gunners, front and rear!

And if a man must have a wife
   She's just the girl I'd pick for life.
Our wedding day you'll see a joke!
   You think we'd drive like common folk!

Or march like infantry! No, no,
   A gunner's wife must make a show;
We'll gallop on the gun to church
   And she'll not leave me in the lurch!

The Bandit

The clouds are hanging, hanging low,
   And mists are drifting slow
Where, dim as shadows, o'er the plain
   Twelve bandits softly go.

      (The clouds are hanging, hanging low,
      And mists are drifting slow).

Of gun and dagger intertwined
   That stretcher rude they bear,
Low voices clamour round their chief
   Who lies so tranquil there.

      (The clouds are hanging, hanging low,
      And mists are drifting slow).

"Tell us your thoughts, brave Ataman,"
   Why do you silent lie
With wide eyes staring at the mist!
   Why do you not reply?"

      (The clouds are hanging, hanging low,
      And mists are drifting slow).

"Tell us your thoughts, brave Ataman."
   More urgent now they call:
Then close the eyes that see no more
   The mist that is his pall.

      (The clouds are hanging, hanging low,
      And mists are drifting slow).

The Conscript

At dawn, my dearest ones, we say farewell,
   Long, long the lonely years!
Farewell, my dearest ones, farewell, farewell,
   The dawn shall come with tears.

      Farewell, my dearest ones, farewell, farewell,
      The dawn shall come with tears.

The morn shall shine upon my mother's grief,
   My sister's weeping eyes,
Oh! father, brother, mourn not now,
   On tears the sun shall rise.

      Farewell, my dearest ones, farewell, farewell,
      The dawn shall come with tears.

Come near my love, my own, the night is ours,
   Lie closer to my heart:
Let darkness give you to my arms
   For daylight bids us part.

      Farewell, my dearest ones, farewell, farewell,
      The dawn shall come with tears.

For me the marching feet, the trumpet call,
   For you the empty years,
For me the roar of guns, the fight,
   For you the silent tears.

      Farewell, my dearest ones, farewell, farewell,
      The dawn shall come with tears.

To Her First Love

Still in the desolate and secret night
my heart unrolls a hidden tapestry
whose warp and woof of rich embroideries
were woven in the pattern of our love.

Out of the shadowy fabric of the past
the jewelled moments kindle one by one
like spectral stars that quicken into life
to glow with such remembered ecstasy
that all our days and nights are galaxies
within the heaven of its brightest fold.
It should have ended here, my web with yours,
death should have been a star-bright moment too
set in high symmetry of light and shade
for had I shared the dark I had not known
the long grey brooding of the twilight gloom.
Why did this heart so amorous of death
yet fail to die?

        See how ironic life
Has torn our gleaming stitchery to shreds
and chains me to its unrelenting loom
Where I must weave dull homespun to the last.

So in the desolate and secret night
I quench my star-bright moments one by one.

Love's Finest Hour

Stale and monotonous the tideless sea,
they know not love whose love would changeless be:
Strong flow, wide ebb keep salt the ocean's breath,
that which is changeless is not love but death.

Let love grow on to love as youth to age
and every heart-throb turn a different page
where on new whiteness love shall write his name.
Heart's fire burns longer than its beating flame:
Kindled at first by fancy's wayward spark
it spreads unseen within the spirit's dark
till tongues of living light unfold, devour
all reek of passion. Then love's finest hour
shall bid bright embers glow to warm and bless,
pure fire upon an altar's holiness.

FIDELITY

Let me be true to all of those I love
Nor ever ask them if they be true to me:
The faithful have their faith, it is the false
Who have the most need of my fidelity.

To Her Last Love

Self-prisoned in the ruin of lost years
I set a flower beside each scattered stone
that I might make a garden of a tomb
where memory and I shall dwell alone.

Safe in the polished armour of a smile
(for smiles like roses grow on many a grave)
I bartered all the blossoms of my pain
and in my coat of mail I passed for brave.

But when you came I tore up by the roots
the gaudy blooms that hid the buried years
and gave you truth for truth. So wept no more
into my secret, useless well of tears.

I have rebuilt the temple of my soul:
Its jewelled windows paint the sunlit air
its quiet cloisters shelter healing peace
that you may come and find refreshment there.

And I have cleansed my heart of all its griefs
that I may dedicate myself anew
to tend my altar-flame of loving faith
and keep it burning day and night for you.

Discord

We walked in the land of faery
    my love and I
the voice of the wind was music –
    of earth? of sky?

A taut string snapt by a rude touch –
    my love's? my own?
and out of the land of faery
    I stepped – alone.

To a Barrage Balloon

We used to say "If pigs could fly!"
    And now they do.
I saw one sailing in the sky
Some thousand feet above his sty,
    A fat one, too!
I scarcely could believe my eyes,
So just imagine my surprise
To see so corpulent a pig
Inconsequently dance a jig
    Upon a cloud.
And, when elated by the show
I clapped my hands and called "Bravo!"
    He turned and bowed.
Then, all at once, he seemed to flop
And dived behind a chimney-top
    Out of my sight.
"He's down" thought I; but not at all,
'Twas only pride that had the fall:
    To my delight
He rose, quite gay and debonair,
Resolved to go on dancing there
    Both day and night.

    So pigs can fly,
    They really do,
This chap, though anchored in the slime,
Could reach an altitude sublime –
    A pig, 'tis true!
    I wish I knew
Just how not only pigs but men
Might rise to nobler heights again
    Right in the blue
    And start anew!

Wings

Shuttle of thought, traffic of flying things:
a bird, a butterfly, a honey-bee
and, high above the spire-crowned lilac tree,
a bomber plane. Tireless the brown bee clings
packing his merchandise, the blackbird brings
beak-load on beak-load to his family,
the butterfly makes love, white-robed, carefree;
the plane brings death on shining silver wings.

Survival's gifts: the bee's fine armoured sting,
the beak that's curved to slay as well as sing,
the urge that prompts the butterfly to steal
a cabbage-leaf to give her child a meal;
but whence, that man may man annihilate,
synthetic wings and scientific hate?

We May Not Sing – We Dare Not Sleep

Unquiet are the shadowy halls of sleep,
the velvet stillness slashed and torn with pain:
nor tourniquet can stem the spreading stain
(flood-tide of agony) the while we reap
the bitter whirlwind who have sown so deep
the scornful wind. Fertile the lethal grain
scarce scattered till we harvest it again,
green corn of youth to stack a rubbish-heap.

Ironic task! To gather figs from thorns
and from a score of wrongs to conjure right.
Only the birds have songs for April morns
beasts find the soft, enfolding arms of night:
we may not sing that have forgotten how,
we dare not sleep whose dreams are haunted now.

Blitzed

All down our street
the houses have no eyes
no shining friendly glass
to greet me as I pass.

Grim company.
Dark, cavernous sockets in a skull,
aloof, indifferent and dull.
They once had eyes that smiled. Like me
they shed their facile, useless tears;
but now – no hopes, no fears.

 One last wild look –
(What horrors did they see
in that eternity?)
One shuddering cry of terror and surprise
when hell's winged hate drove heaven from the skies,
blasting and burning, every sulphurous breath
screaming of death.

All down our street
where houses have no eyes;
bereft of sight,
with hands outstretched as in a cave
I grope for light.
The windows of my mind,
shuttered so well, are blasted too and blind,
black with despair:
and how shall I grow wise
that have no eyes?

With Beak and Claw

Blacker than carrion crows,
the whole world's woes
flock round to pick the bare bones of my joy,
and what they crave destroy.
Tearing with beak and claw,
their clamour of distress
proclaims my emptiness
and fills no hungry craw.

There was a place
in Once-upon-a-time
when hearts would sing
till benediction spilled its golden rain
on everything:
when laughter was a scarecrow,
and the earth
rippled and rioted
with flowers of mirth.

But hearts are silent now
and laughter dumb:
from east and west
the dark-winged starvelings come
to perch on laughter's shoulder,
peck his eyes,
and gorge their grief where joy unguarded lies.
Beauty has gone.
See how the flowers of mirth
wither and rot upon the barren earth,
no bright thought sings,
no benizon is shed,
now joy is dead.

LIFE'S NEW YEAR

Out of night's deepest shadow
    dawn's bright spear
leaps to the new day's conflict
    sharp and clear.
Cleaving despair and darkness,
    hope is near,
drawn from its sheath to challenge
    life's new year.

    Out of the womb of pain
    joy shall be born again.

Easter – 1946

Green of the waking woodlands
light on the face of spring
joy in the dancing sunbeam
music of birds that sing
fragrance of hidden violets
bright peals of daffodils
wanderlust of shadows
that race across the hills
glory of sudden rainbows
painting the cloud's quick tears
and God's love cleansing the heart of man
for the healing of the years.

Oneless

Creator and creature are one,
With pale, multitudinous hands
they carry their blessing – or curse –
to the heirs of the ultimate lands.
Death always implicit in life
as joy is enfolded in pain,
light breaking its chrysalis dark
to find a winged glory again.
The tree that is born of the fruit
gives life to the fruit of the tree,
the man still the child that he was,
the child now the man that shall be.
The morning that burns in the east
is evening a-flame in the west,
for one are the day and the night
for one are the worst and the best.
The first and the last shall be one,
the end the beginning as well,
twin blossomings – evil and good,
twin harvestings – Heaven and Hell.

The Poet
for J.H.

Thoughts, turbulent as sea-birds in their flight,
explore the dizzy labyrinth of mind
with urgent, hungry cries: their quest to find
hid in an unplumbed depth, an unscaled height,
some mirrored splendour of the Infinite,
sun of the path and messenger combined
whose aery escalators intertwined
weave ever-changing filigrees of light.

Within, without the strange kaleidoscope,
child of his wonder, parent of his hope,
the poet, quickened by creative fire,
moulding the pattern which his thoughts inspire,
finds hot words hardening in cool delays,
his soul's salvation balanced on a phrase.

The Talisman
for D.I.

Soul's breathes not a word more sweet than friend:
its cadence falls as falls a melody
from wings that soar, undaunted, strong and free.
Its light to sorrow's dark its radiance lend,
its wealth to bankrupt hope give more to spend,
it is the talisman upon life's sea,
nor ocean's lure nor port's tranquillity
can dull its shining till the voyage end.

So call me friend and from my heart shall flow
such warmth as shall persuade your own to know
what precious alchemy this word can hold
to take our dross and turn it all to gold.
Let there be ugliness or doubt or fear,
we'll make them beauty, faith and courage here.

To the Author of *Flowers for a Lady*

So tender are the pale blooms of your song,
petal and leaf
twined by a poet's grief,
I turn each page with gentle reverent hand
trying to understand
how life may be a crucible of pain
transmuting love and joy and youth
to fine pure gold of truth:
shaping a heart's quick tears,
flowing from stony years
through subterranean caves of haunted dark,
to lyric beauty crystalline and rare
that all may share.

Because you gave your sorrow for our gain
these shining flowers of living light
grown in the corridors of night
must gleam and glow
with radiance that joy's blossoms never know:
love gleaned from death shall deathless be
the rose that crowns your elegy.

The Path and the Goal

I have wandered too long in the dark wood
on the labyrinthian path.
Where truth has fled
it lured and led,
it twisted and turned and twined
till the beckoning song of the bright-winged bird
that implores the sky
is the baffled cry
of the beast left far behind:
for the path of thought is the no-path
to the ever-darkening west
and it cannot lead to the goal
for the goal is lost in the quest.

Silent

Death has no words. Stone silent
   You lie and will not speak
While I would read your spirit's need
   On sculptured brow and cheek.

Grief has no light. Tear-blinded
   I grope through baffled pain
To search for flowers of sunlit hours
   That will not bloom again.

Faith's praying hands are lifted:
   Two white wings poised in air
That cannot bless my loneliness
   With love no longer there.

The sea flows wide between us
   And ever by its shore
A dark tide rolls, a lone bell tolls
   "No more, no more, no more."

Elegy

Age has no songs, no wreath of woven words
    to crown her grief,
the naked tree yields to the winter's storm
    not one frail leaf.

Green thoughts for youth, white phrase for elegy
    when hearts love on,
let silence build her monument of stone
    when love has gone.

ALONE

I know that I must always be alone
prisoned within my self-spun sphere of glass;
so many faces come, so many pass,
yet never one that I may claim my own.

For these, too, spin their tenuous cocoons,
transparent fortresses where souls may hide.
Alone, alone! Forever we abide
shackled, on winter nights, on summer noons.

Near is too far. Though twain should be one flesh
fire in the veins leaves ice to freeze the heart.
Lips cling to lips while spirits mourn apart,
no net so fine but self slips through the mesh.

Craving the truth, the truth we may not tell!
"All that I have is yours" each cries to each,
hiding the dearest treasure out of reach.
Alone we come, alone we say farewell.

Milestone

I have made friends with age. Why should I weep
that I have walked so far – the way I came
kindled to beauty in the sunset flame,
youth's fields still mine, with full-eared corn to reap
Where in the spring the ploughshare furrowed deep,
gleanings of love (a richer yield than fame)
blessing from lips that softly speak my name,
and evening's tender radiance till I sleep.

Seed-time and harvest of the spirit's year:
is this the cycle? is the ending here?
Or, having slept, do souls awake once more
to live and love and labour as before.
If there be fresh adventure I'll find zest,
if sleep be all, I am content to rest.

Farewell

Farewell is not a word to speak with tears,
I'll say it with a smile.
This smouldering torch will flare a little while,
kindling to gladness like an autumn wood
wearing the sun's last kiss,
knowing farewell is this –
To light the beeches' bonfires
and to stand
scattering with lavish hand
the hoarded guineas of the birches' store
till there not one more.

Farewell!
Gay as the autumn leaves
the banners courage weaves :
I'll hang their flimsy, fluttering red and gold
on walls of cold, gray stone,
to deck the gateway leading to the path
where you shall walk alone.

Farewell!
Now let the neutral landscape of the years
erase the memory
and dull the dream:
no hill-top shall be misty with my tears
no valley sad with sighing winds that tell
how dark the shadow of this bright farewell.

The Rope

A phantom rope, a shadow on the gray,
moored fast to nothingness. The sullen sea,
secret, fog-burdened, with a pledge for me:
somewhere a ship, somewhere a landing lay.
A sea-bird's crying in a shrouded bay,
a soul's voice tearing at the mystery
of all that was and all that was to be,
what sun, what storm, what blue of summer day!

Veiled source, veiled destiny. Yet taut the span
of twisted cable where the life of man
binds each to each. The hand that made the rope
created a creator and a hope:
God-man, man-God, an endless unity
the ship, the rope, the landing and the sea.

Acknowledgements

My thanks to publisher Alan Hayes of Arlen House for his professionalism and his deep commitment to the publication of women's writing, Thanks too, to Gillian MacIntosh who first alerted me to the poetry of May Morton, to Dr Tina O'Toole and Prof Joseph O'Connor for their generous guidance and support, to Anne Stewart of the Ulster Museum who unearthed the portrait which is reproduced on the cover of this book. To my colleagues in the WEB group and in Irish PEN/PEN na hÉireann for their solidarity over the years and, most of all, with thanks to May Morton herself who left a legacy of poetry and whose work for Irish PEN has endured.

About the Author

May Morton (1879–1957) was born in Limerick. As a young woman she moved to Northern Ireland where she was a teacher in, and subsequently became vice-principal of, The Girls Model School, Belfast. In 1936, *Dawn and Afterglow,* her first poetry collection, was published, followed by *Masque in Maytime* (1948) and *Sung to the Spinning Wheel* (1952), her final poetry collection. *Spindle and Shuttle,* her 200 line poem about the Belfast mill workers, won her the prestigious Festival of Britain, Northern Ireland Prize in 1951. She was a central figure in the Belfast Centre of Irish PEN.

About the Editor

Liz McManus is a novelist and short story writer. Awards include Listowel, Irish Pen (Short Story awards) and Hennessy Award (New Irish Writing). Novels: *Acts of Subversion* (Poolbeg 1991) was shortlisted for the Aer Lingus/*Irish Times* award; *A Shadow in the Yard* (Ward River Press, 2013), *When Things Come to Light* (Arlen House 2023). Elected to Dail Éireann in 1992, she was Minister of State for Housing and Urban Renewal (1994–97). Chair of the Commission on the Needs of Travellers and a long-time campaigner for women's rights. She has an MPhil, Creative Writing (TCD, 2012) and PhD (Creative Writing) (UL, 2024).